A DATE WHICH WILL LIVE IN INFAMY

ATTACK ON PEARL HARBOR

Virginia Loh-Hagan

45th Parallel Press

Published in the United States of America by Cherry Lake Publishing
Ann Arbor, Michigan
www.cherrylakepublishing.com

Reading Adviser: Marla Conn MS, Ed., Literacy specialist, Read-Ability, Inc.
Book Designer: Felicia Macheske

Photo Credits: © Keith Tarrier/Shutterstock.com, cover, 1; Harris & Ewing, Library of Congress, LC-DIG-hec-47601, 5; © V.L. Winter/Shutterstock.com, 6; © jgorzynik/Shutterstock.com, 11; Library of Congress, LC-USW33-018433-C, 12; © Everett Historical/Shutterstock.com, 17, 23; © David Carillet/Shutterstock.com, 18; © Kevin M. McCarthy/Shutterstock.com, 21; Photo: NH 54564, Courtesy U. S. Naval History and Heritage Command, Pearl Harbor Navy Yard February 5, 1942, (Public Domain) 25; Library of Congress, LC-USZ62-133629, 29

Graphic Elements Throughout: © Chipmunk131/Shutterstock.com; © Nowik Sylwia/Shutterstock.com; © Andrey_Popov/Shutterstock.com; © NadzeyaShanchuk/Shutterstock.com; © KathyGold/Shutterstock.com; © Black creator/Shutterstock.com; © Edvard Molnar/Shutterstock.com; © Elenadesign/Shutterstock.com; © estherpoon/Shutterstock.com

45th Parallel Press is an imprint of Cherry Lake Publishing.

Library of Congress Cataloging-in-Publication Data

Names: Loh-Hagan, Virginia, author.
Title: A Date which will live in infamy : attack on Pearl Harbor / by Virginia Loh-Hagan.
Description: Ann Arbor : Cherry Lake Publishing, 2019. | Series: Behind the curtain | Includes bibliographical references and index.
Identifiers: LCCN 2018035570| ISBN 9781534143425 (hardcover) | ISBN 9781534141186 (pdf) | ISBN 9781534139985 (pbk.) | ISBN 9781534142381 (hosted ebook)
Subjects: LCSH: Pearl Harbor (Hawaii), Attack on, 1941—Juvenile literature.
Classification: LCC D767.92 .L59 2019 | DDC 940.54/26693—dc23
LC record available at https://lccn.loc.gov/2018035570

Cherry Lake Publishing would like to acknowledge the work of The Partnership for 21st Century Skills. Please visit www.p21.org for more information.

Printed in the United States of America
Corporate Graphics

A Note on Dramatic Retellings

Participating in Readers Theater, or dramatic retellings, can greatly improve reading skills, especially fluency. The books in the **BEHIND THE CURTAIN** series give readers opportunities to learn about important historical events in a fun and engaging way. These books serve as a bridge to more complex texts. All the characters are real figures from history; however, their stories have been fictionalized. To learn more about the people and the events, check out the Viewpoints and Perspectives series and the Perspectives Library series, as the **BEHIND THE CURTAIN** books are aligned to these stories.

TABLE of CONTENTS

HiSTORICAL BACKGROUND

Sunday, December 7, 1941, is "a date which will live in infamy," said U.S. president Franklin D. Roosevelt. On this date, Japan attacked Pearl Harbor. It took the United States by surprise.

At this time, much of Europe and Asia were fighting in World War II. Japan needed oil for military tanks and ships. It attacked countries in Asia to get their oil. It didn't want the United States to defend these countries. It needed to destroy U.S. military power. So, it attacked Pearl Harbor.

Pearl Harbor is a U.S. navy base. It's in the Pacific Ocean. The U.S. Pacific Fleet is there. The fleet is the main military force in the Pacific Ocean.

FLASH FACT!

President Franklin D. Roosevelt's "Day of Infamy" speech took 7 minutes.

Vocabulary

infamy (IN-fuh-mee) known everywhere for an extremely bad thing

fleet (FLEET) a group of naval ships

FLASH FACT!

Japan surrendered aboard the USS Missouri *on September 2, 1945.*

Vocabulary

torpedoes (tor-PEE-dohz)
underwater missiles or bombs

Japanese submarines fired torpedoes. Japanese planes dropped bombs. Japan's attack lasted 2 hours and 20 minutes. The Japanese sank or damaged 21 U.S. navy ships. They destroyed or damaged over 300 U.S. planes. Over 2,400 Americans died. Nearly 1,200 people were hurt.

The attack on Pearl Harbor woke up the "sleeping giant." The United States didn't want to get involved in the war. But the events of December 7 couldn't go unpunished.

The next day, America declared war on Japan. It entered World War II. It won in 1945. It sank the Japanese ships that attacked Pearl Harbor.

CAST of CHARACTERS

NARRATOR: person who helps tell the story

TAKESHI MAEDA: Japanese navy pilot sent to attack Pearl Harbor

ISHI TANAKA: Japanese navy pilot sent to attack Pearl Harbor

MIRIAM HOP: wife of Harvey Hop and daughter of a U.S. Army officer

HARVEY HOP: U.S. Navy pilot **stationed** at Pearl Harbor and husband of Miriam Hop

ROBERT VARILL: U.S. Navy fireman stationed at Pearl Harbor

RONALD CARTER: U.S. Marine stationed at Pearl Harbor

ALANI ONAJEA: **native** Hawaiian who works near Pearl Harbor

FRANKLIN D. ROOSEVELT: U.S. president during this time

BACKSTORY
SPOTLIGHT BIOGRAPHY

Rudy Martinez was from San Diego. He was a Mexican American. He was a high school wrestling champion. He was a boxer. He joined the navy. He was an electrician. He became a sailor. He was 21 years old when he left for Pearl Harbor. He set sail on the USS *Utah*. All of a sudden, there was a loud boom. The Japanese attacked. Two torpedoes hit the ship. The ship quickly began to sink. Martinez was trapped inside. He died. He was the first Hispanic to be killed in World War II. Six officers and 52 other men also died in the ship. Martinez was given medals after his death. Before he died, he wrote a letter to his mother. He asked for her picture.

Vocabulary

stationed (STAY-shuhnd) assigned to a place

native (NAY-tiv) someone who is born and raised in a certain place

FLASH FACT!

Japan's kamikaze pilots crashed their planes into their targets. They killed themselves by doing so.

ACT 1

NARRATOR: *It's November 27, 1941. Japanese warships are leaving Japan.* **TAKESHI MAEDA** *and* **ISHI TANAKA** *are Japanese pilots. They're on an* **aircraft carrier**.

TAKESHI: Where are we going?

ISHI: Pearl Harbor.

TAKESHI: Why are we going to Pearl Harbor? We don't want a war with the U.S.

ISHI: The U.S. banned trade with us. We can't fight other countries without oil. We need oil for our tanks and planes. We need to build our **empire**. We can't let the U.S. stop us from doing that. We have to stop them first.

TAKESHI: Do you think we're going to win? The U.S. is very powerful.

ISHI: We're taking them by surprise. Plus, we have a large fleet. We have six aircraft carriers. We have 420 planes. We have battleships. We have **tanker ships**. We have **submarines**.

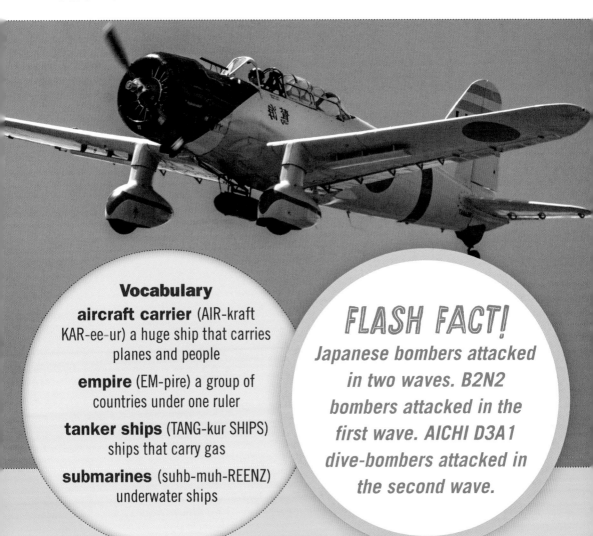

Vocabulary

aircraft carrier (AIR-kraft KAR-ee-ur) a huge ship that carries planes and people

empire (EM-pire) a group of countries under one ruler

tanker ships (TANG-kur SHIPS) ships that carry gas

submarines (suhb-muh-REENZ) underwater ships

FLASH FACT!

Japanese bombers attacked in two waves. B2N2 bombers attacked in the first wave. AICHI D3A1 dive-bombers attacked in the second wave.

TAKESHI: But why Pearl Harbor?

ISHI: The U.S. has many ships and planes there. If we bomb it, then the U.S. won't be able to fight us later. We have to destroy their military power. Maybe this will stop a bigger war.

TAKESHI: It's too bad we have to attack. I wish **Emperor** Hirohito and President Roosevelt could have worked out a peace deal.

ISHI: Me too. But that isn't the case. And we must do our **duty**.

TAKESHI: Japan is a small country. We need resources. The U.S. is trying to hurt us. We have no choice. We must **strike** first.

NARRATOR: *The Japanese fleet traveled for several days. They got to Pearl Harbor on Sunday, December 7, 1941.* **TAKESHI** *and* **ISHI** *are flying their* **bombers***. They're talking on their radios.*

Vocabulary
emperor (EM-pur-ur) the leader of an empire
duty (DOO-tee) job
strike (STRIKE) to hit or attack
bombers (BAH-murz) planes that drop bombs

FLASH FACT!
Ships at Pearl Harbor were close together. Damage on one ship quickly spread to other ships.

TAKESHI: I see it! I see a long white line of **coast**.

ISHI: That must be the Hawaiian islands.

TAKESHI: I'm going to make a loop around.

ISHI: Is anyone there?

TAKESHI: Pearl Harbor sleeps. No one knows we're here.

ISHI: I just got the orders. It's 7:55 a.m. Bombs away!

TAKESHI: Swoop low. Fire!

ISHI: **Tora**! Tora! Tora!

TAKESHI: Tiger? Why are you saying tiger?

ISHI: That's our code word. It means that we've **succeeded**. We did a surprise attack. The U.S. never saw us coming. Submarines hit their battleships from underwater. We hit them from above.

TAKESHI: What have we done? Now, we are at war with the U.S.

LOCATION SHOOTING
REAL-WORLD SETTING

Pearl Harbor is on the island of Oahu, Hawaii. It's west of Honolulu. It's the largest natural harbor in Hawaii. It's a place where ships can be docked. It's a U.S. Navy base. It's the main offices of the U.S. Pacific Fleet. Its Hawaiian name means "long hill." Hawaiian stories say it's the home of the shark god and goddess. Pearl Harbor was named for the pearl oysters found there. Today, Pearl Harbor is home to five historic sites. The most famous is the USS *Arizona* Memorial. The USS *Arizona* was a battleship. It was attacked by the Japanese. A memorial was built where the battleship sank. The battleship sank in 9 minutes, and 1,177 people died.

Vocabulary

coast (KOHST) the edge of the land near the sea

tora (TOR-uh) Japanese word for tiger

succeeded (suhk-SEED-id) gotten the job done, won

FLASH FACT!
Chuichi Nagumo oversaw the Japanese attack on Pearl Harbor.

NARRATOR: **MIRIAM** and **HARVEY HOP** *live near Pearl Harbor. They wake up to a loud booming sound.*

MIRIAM: What was that? I just felt the house shake.

HARVEY: It sounds like an **explosion**. Something must be happening at Pearl Harbor.

MIRIAM: Could it be a **drill**? Hurry! Look out the window. Can you see anything?

HARVEY: Miriam . . .

MIRIAM: What's wrong? What do you see?

HARVEY: It's smoke. It's coming from Hickam **Airfield**.

MIRIAM: Oh no! That's where the fighter planes and fuel tanks are. The whole place could catch fire!

HARVEY: A fire would be a **disaster**. We can't lose our planes!

MIRIAM: The air is getting smoky. Look at the clouds of smoke. They're filling the sky!

HARVEY: Wait! I also see smoke at Pearl Harbor. Oh no . . .

MIRIAM: What is it, Harvey?

Vocabulary

explosion (ik-SPLOH-zhuhn) blowing apart of something caused by a bomb

drill (DRIL) practice

airfield (AIR-feeld) a place where planes are stored

disaster (dih-ZAS-tur) an event that causes great damage or loss

FLASH FACT!

There were 51 planes at Hickam Airfield. Half were destroyed or damaged.

HARVEY: I think we're being attacked.

MIRIAM: Attacked? We've stayed out of that war in Europe and Asia. Why would anyone want to attack us?

HARVEY: Look out the window. See those planes? See the signs on the wings?

MIRIAM: Are you talking about the red circles? They look like meatballs.

HARVEY: Those are Japanese planes.

NARRATOR: *The Hops hear another loud bang.*

MIRIAM: Harvey! Did you hear that?

HARVEY: That Japanese plane just hit one of our planes.

MIRIAM: This can't be happening! I can see the Japanese pilot!

HARVEY: I have to get to the **base**. This looks like an **air strike**.

Vocabulary

base (BASE) a place owned and operated by the military

air strike (AIR STRIKE) an attack by planes dropping bombs from the air

FLASH FACT!

Japan is known as the land of the rising sun. Their symbol looks like a red circle.

ACT 2

NARRATOR: *Japanese bombers circle the sky. They're dropping bombs.* **TAKESHI** *and* **ISHI** *talk over the radio.*

TAKESHI: Did you see that? That was a big crash!

ISHI: That was one of our planes. It just hit the U.S. plane.

TAKESHI: The pilot is having a hard time starting his plane again.

ISHI: He fixed it. There he goes. But wait . . .

TAKESHI: His plane is crashing. He's hitting that building. He's going to die.

ISHI: There are people in that building. Not all those people are soldiers. Now, they're all going to die.

TAKESHI: This is war. War is unfair. Nobody wins. We can only hope for **honorable** deaths.

ISHI: Did we do the right thing?

TAKESHI: We did what our country asked of us. We did our job.

Vocabulary
honorable (AH-nur-uh-buhl)
with honor

FLASH FACT!
Twenty-nine Japanese planes were shot down by U.S. soldiers.

NARRATOR: *Soldiers are running around Pearl Harbor.*
HARVEY HOP *arrives in a panic and finds* **ROBERT VARILL.**

HARVEY: What's going on?

ROBERT: **Air raid** on Pearl Harbor. This is not a drill. **Battleship Row** has been hit! The *Arizona* exploded.

HARVEY: What happened?

ROBERT: The Japanese hit the weapons room. There was an explosion. It ripped a hole in the side of the ship. Then it took three more hits. The ship went down in minutes. Over 1,000 crew members were trapped. They all died.

HARVEY: Some of my friends were on that ship. How can I help?

ROBERT: We must hurry. Oil is leaking out of the ships. I'll pull the **survivors** out of the water. You can take the hurt soldiers to the hospital ship, *Solace*.

HARVEY: Let's save as many lives as we can.

Vocabulary

air raid (AIR RAYD) an attack done by planes

Battleship Row (BAT-uhl-ship ROH) a group of warships in Pearl Harbor

survivors (sur-VYE-vurz) people who live through a bad event

FLASH FACT!
The USS Arizona was hit four times before sinking.

NARRATOR: *On the hospital ship, there are many hurt soldiers.* **RONALD CARTER** *is one of them.* **MIRIAM HOP** *is on the ship, too. She is one of many* **volunteers**.

MIRIAM: Let me clean your burns. What happened?

RONALD: I was on the *Arizona*. I woke up. I went to the dining hall. I heard the ship's **siren**. I ran to my **battle station**. I thought it was a drill.

MIRIAM: We all did.

RONALD: I heard a loud blast. The ship was hit. It was sinking. I jumped into the water. Some men were trapped. They drowned with the ship.

Vocabulary

volunteers (vah-luhn-TEERZ) helpers

siren (SYE-ruhn) alarm

battle station (BAT-uhl STAY-shuhn) a place where soldiers can shoot guns at enemies

FLASH FACT!

Except for three ships, every damaged ship was fixed and returned to sea.

MIRIAM: How did you get here?

RONALD: Someone pulled me from the water. Another person brought me to this hospital. His name was Hop.

MIRIAM: Harvey Hop?

RONALD: Yes! You know him?

MIRIAM: That's my husband.

RONALD: He's a hero.

MIRIAM: So are you.

NARRATOR: *It's December 8, 1941. People are gathering near the radio.* **MIRIAM HOP** *joins* **ALANI ONAJEA**. *They are waiting to hear a speech by President* **FRANKLIN D. ROOSEVELT**.

MIRIAM: Did I miss it?

ALANI: No. We still have a couple of minutes before he speaks.

MIRIAM: Thanks for volunteering at the hospital with me.

ALANI: No problem. I'm glad I can. It is sad to see all these hurt and dying men. Helping makes me feel good.

MIRIAM: Turn the radio up. President Roosevelt is speaking.

PRESIDENT ROOSEVELT: Yesterday, December 7th, 1941, a date which will live in infamy, the United States of America was suddenly and **deliberately** attacked by naval and air forces of the Empire of Japan.

ALANI: I still can't believe it happened.

BLOOPERS
HISTORICAL MISTAKES

Timing is everything. Japan attacked on a Sunday morning. This took the United States by surprise. It was not prepared for an attack. In this way, Japan had good timing. But, in other ways, Japan had bad timing. Nine out of 10 soldiers weren't at Pearl Harbor. They were ashore. They were on leave. Sundays are usually days of rest. This means Japan didn't kill as many men as it wanted to. Japan chose to attack on December 7, 1941. It carefully picked this date. But many aircraft carriers weren't in Pearl Harbor. They were out to sea. They were on missions. They missed the attack. This meant that they were ready for battle. Japan didn't destroy the U.S. Navy. Many U.S. lives were lost. But thanks to Japan's poor timing, the United States still had more men, ships, and weapons.

Vocabulary
deliberately (dih-LIB-ur-it-lee)
on purpose

FLASH FACT!
Most Americans learned of the Pearl Harbor attack on December 8, 1941.

PRESIDENT ROOSEVELT: I **regret** to tell you that very many American lives have been lost.

MIRIAM: I'm grateful to have Harvey with me. But my heart breaks for those who will never return home.

PRESIDENT ROOSEVELT: I ask that the Congress declare war between the United States and the Japanese empire.

ALANI: So, we're now a nation at war.

MIRIAM: The Japanese attacked us without declaring war first. This was a sneak attack. We have to fight back.

ALANI: These are scary times. What if there's another attack on Pearl Harbor? We're under **martial law**. We're going to have **blackouts** every night. There's talk about sending Japanese Americans to **internment** camps. There are a lot of Japanese Americans in Hawaii. They're loyal. But people think they're spies. It's not fair.

MIRIAM: War is not fair. Nobody wins.

Vocabulary

regret (rih-GRET) feeling sorry

martial law (MAHR-shuhl LAW) direct military control

blackouts (BLAK-outs) programs in which people turn off lights to make the city look dark so it can't be seen and attacked

internment (in-TURN-muhnt) the forced relocation of a group of people

FLASH FACT!
Once the United States declared war, troops were sent abroad to fight.

EVENT TIMELINE

July 1937: Japan wants to become an empire. It invades North China.

July 1940: The United States wants to stop Japan. It stops trading with Japan.

January 1941: Admiral Isoroku Yamamoto leads Japan's navy. He begins talking about attacking Pearl Harbor.

January 27, 1941: Joseph C. Grew is the U.S. ambassador to Japan. He contacts U.S. leaders. He tells them about Japan's attack plans. Nobody believes him.

April 1941: U.S. officers spy on the Japanese. They decode secret messages.

May 1941: A Japanese officer tells his leaders that the United States is reading his messages. No one believes him.

Summer 1941: Yamamoto trains his soldiers. He makes final plans for his attack.

September 24, 1941: The United States decodes a message. Japanese leaders are asking for exact locations of ships in Pearl Harbor. This information is not shared with Hawaii's military leaders.

November 16, 1941: Submarines leave Japan. They head to Pearl Harbor.

November 26, 1941: Japanese aircraft carriers and other ships head to Pearl Harbor.

November 27, 1941: Washington, D.C., sends a warning to U.S. military leaders in Hawaii. They tell them there may be an attack from Japan.

December 6, 1941: The United States decodes a message about a Pearl Harbor attack. The message is sent to leaders in Hawaii after the attack begins.

December 7, 1941: Japanese planes attack Pearl Harbor. They attack the ships in the harbor. They attack nearby military bases.

December 8, 1941: President Franklin D. Roosevelt addresses Congress. He asks for a declaration of war against Japan. Congress approves, and the country enters World War II.

CONSIDER THIS!

TAKE A POSITION! The United States didn't like what Japan was doing to China. Should America have gotten involved with Japan's war with China? Argue your point with reasons and evidence.

SAY WHAT? Read President Franklin D. Roosevelt's "Infamy Speech." This is one of the most famous speeches. Explain what it means. Explain why it's important.

THINK ABOUT IT! The attack on Pearl Harbor pushed America into World War II. What if it hadn't happened? What if the United States hadn't fought in the war? How different do you think the world would be? *The Man in the High Castle* is a book. It's by Philip K. Dick. It's an alternate history. Alternate means another version. The book imagines Japan and Germany as winners of the war. Write your own alternate history about Pearl Harbor.

LEARN MORE

Allen, Thomas B. *Remember Pearl Harbor: American and Japanese Survivors Tell Their Storie*s. Washington, DC: National Geographic Children's Books, 2015.

Demuth, Patricia Brennan. *What Was Pearl Harbor?* New York: Penguin, 2013.

Krieg, Katherine. *The Attack on Pearl Harbor.* Ann Arbor, MI: Cherry Lake Publishing, 2014.

Owens, Lisa L. *Attack on Pearl Harbor.* Minneapolis: Lerner Group, 2018.

Russo, Kristin J. *Viewpoints on the Attack on Pearl Harbor.* Ann Arbor, MI: Cherry Lake Publishing, 2019.

INDEX

ABOUT THE AUTHOR

Dr. Virginia Loh-Hagan is an author, university professor, and former classroom teacher. Her godson, Felix, grew up near Pearl Harbor, Hawaii. This book is dedicated to him. She lives in San Diego with her very tall husband and very naughty dogs. To learn more about her, visit www.virginialoh.com.